PRIVATE LESSONS

Funk GUITAR
THE ESSENTIAL GUIDE

by ROSS BOLTON

To access audio, visit:
www.halleonard.com/mylibrary

Enter Code
7572-0872-8124-3917

ISBN 978-0-634-01168-9

7777 W. BLUEMOUND RD. P.O. BOX 13819 MILWAUKEE, WI 53213

Visit Hal Leonard Online at
www.halleonard.com

About the Author

Based in Southern California, Ross Bolton is currently a regular member of Al Jarreau's band and has recorded or performed with Rick Braun, David Benoit, The Beach Boys, Sheena Easton, Jeffery Osborne, Nell Carter, Donny Osmond, and many others.

A few of Ross' TV and movie credits include "Everybody Loves Raymond," "The Larry Sanders Show," "Fridays," "Two Guys, a Girl & a Pizza Place," "Casper," Switch," and "The Jeff Foxworthy Show."

Ross has been on staff at Musicians Institute in Hollywood for many years and has conducted seminars and clinics around the world. His popular video on funk guitar and recent CD-Rom are sold internationally, receiving praise from many major trade publications.

Guitar Player magazine has regularly featured Ross as a guest columnist.

For more information please visit *rossbolton.com*

Acknowledgments

Special thanks to Keith Wyatt, Masaki Toriwa, and everyone at Musicians Institute.

Audio tracks produced by Bernhard Groinig and Ross Bolton. Production assistance by Katrin Lassmann.

Contents

Introduction

At some point in the 1960s, James Brown and his band started an epidemic that would forever change the face of modern music. Their nuclear version of soul and R&B inspired a movement that became known as "funk."

The tradition of funk guitar playing is all about one thing: *groove*. Groove is the holy grail of being "in the pocket," which boils down to finding a great part and locking in with the rhythm section. When it all comes together, magic happens!

This book will get you started with all of the basic techniques and chord knowledge you need to jump into the world of funk and groove guitar. The play-along tracks are a fun, essential element for applying the lessons. You'll be refining your groove as you play along with each example.

Remember, funk is party music. It's meant to be fun—so enjoy the journey!

Ross Bolton

Before You Play...

Here are a few things you should consider before you start jamming:

1) Since the whole idea of funk guitar playing is to get tight with the bass and drums, try to practice with a metronome or a drum machine. If you're using a drum machine, keep the pattern simple (hi-hat plays eighth notes, kick drum on beats 1 and 3, snare on 2 and 4).

2) There is, of course, audio provided for you to play along with the examples in the book. In most cases, each example will be played several times at a "performance" tempo, so you hear the part in context. That will be immediately followed by a slower, "practice" version, isolating the guitar with the drums. If you're working without the audio, a good beginning tempo for most of the examples is around 76-84 bpm. Once you get comfortable, the real groove zone is generally between 84-102 bpm.

3) For now, lose the effects. Distortion, delay, reverb… all that stuff will make it more difficult to hear whether you're playing in time. Once you get your technique together, then start experimenting with a wah-wah pedal, phaser, etc.

4) Finally, check out (if you haven't already) the artists that created and defined the world of funk. A "greatest hits" CD by any of these bands would be worth listening to:

- James Brown
- Earth, Wind & Fire
- Cameo
- Tower of Power

- Sly & The Family Stone
- Parliament/Funkadelic
- Ohio Players
- Prince

Of course, there are many others…

1 Getting Started

Since most funk parts are based on a sixteenth-note subdivision, we'll begin by just scratching muted sixteenths.

With your left hand resting lightly on the fretboard (just enough to mute the strings), begin strumming with your right hand. The example below shows that you begin with a downstroke, alternating four strokes per beat.

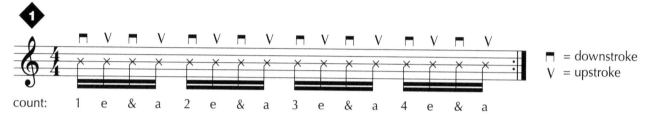

count: 1 e & a 2 e & a 3 e & a 4 e & a

As you play, keep your eye on your strumming hand, and apply these basic rules:

a) Your wrist and arm should be loose! Also, try not to "fix" your fingers or wrist onto the guitar.

b) Don't drag your pick across the strings. Instead, try to make it sound like you're hitting all of the strings at the same time. This will keep your sound tight and focused.

c) At this point, you'll want to always keep your strumming hand moving in time with the music, and keep the volume of all the attacks even like a machine. It's also a good idea to tap your foot as you're playing. And finally...

d) Play strong! This is no time to be shy. If you make a mistake, make a big, loud, ugly mistake.

A word about counting: To keep better time while you play, try tapping your foot once for each beat (1, 2, 3, and 4) and using "e-&-a" to fill out the count, like this: "**one**-ee-and-uh, **two**-ee-and-uh, **three**-ee-and-uh, **four**-ee-and-uh."

2 Divide and Conquer
(Isolating Sixteenths)

Now that you're wailing on the sixteenths, we'll use the ultimate funk chord—E9—to begin playing the attacks. To get the right sound on this voicing, try muting the sixth string with your left-hand thumb so that it doesn't sound. (Note: Throughout this book, the root of the chord will be highlighted.)

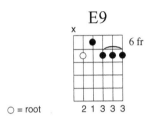

The concept of isolating each of the sixteenths is, without a doubt, the most important element in developing your funk technique. As you play through the following examples, keep the volume of the scratches even with volume of the chord. Also, continue to tap your foot on beats 1, 2, 3, and 4.

Downstrokes: The first and third sixteenth of each beat. The first sixteenth is called the *downbeat*—it's also your tempo or meter. The third sixteenth is called the *upbeat*.

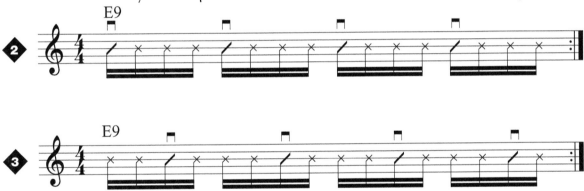

Upstrokes: The second and fourth sixteenth of each beat. Getting the upstrokes "just right" can be tricky. Try to get them as strong as the downstrokes without throwing off the time-feel.

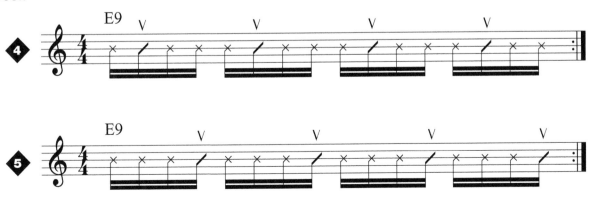

3 Forging the Funk

Now let's combine these sixteenth attacks to create some basic one-bar rhythm patterns. We'll also move around the ninth chord shape to some other keys.

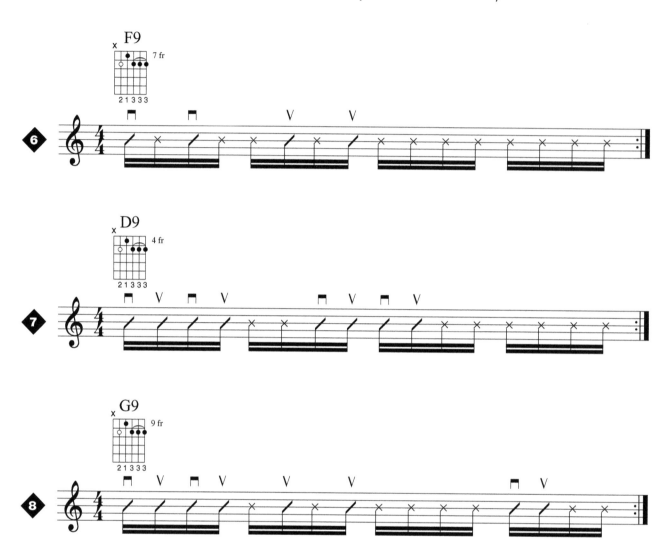

Here's a chord you can use instead of the ninth. Notice that it uses only the top four strings—this type of voicing is typical in funk because it makes the guitar easier to hear among the other instruments.

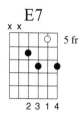

Apply this new E7 shape to the following examples. Focus on the higher strings, and try to avoid hitting the lower strings with your strumming hand!

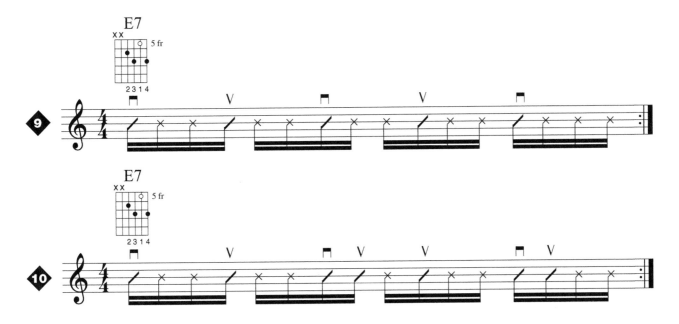

Let's move the same chord shape up three frets to G7.

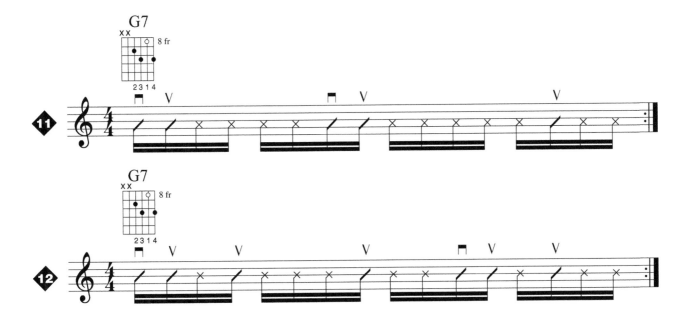

4 Scratch Or Float?

At times, you may want to sustain a chord while you're playing a rhythm pattern, instead of scratching. Although you may be tempted to stop your strumming hand in these instances, it's better to keep that hand moving in the usual sixteenth-note motion, "floating" over the strings as the chord sustains.

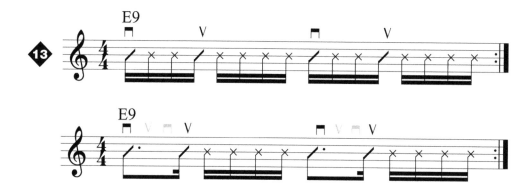

Here's another four-note chord shape, this time in the key of C, with the root on top. Use this shape to play the following example. Be sure to float your hand during the sustained notes.

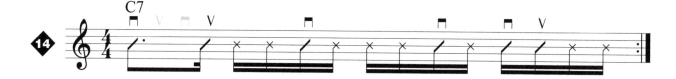

For this pattern, move the same chord shape down three frets to the key of A.

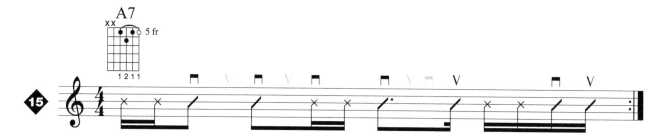

Now try another pattern with this F7 shape.

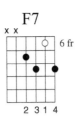

F7

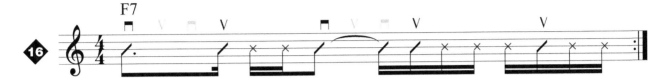

Up to this point, we've been scratching every sixteenth note; this helps keep our time even and our technique more consistent. However, this constant scratching sound isn't always desirable. With the next three rhythm patterns, keep your right hand moving in a normal down/up motion, but strike the strings only on the indicated rhythm—leaving silence between the attacks.

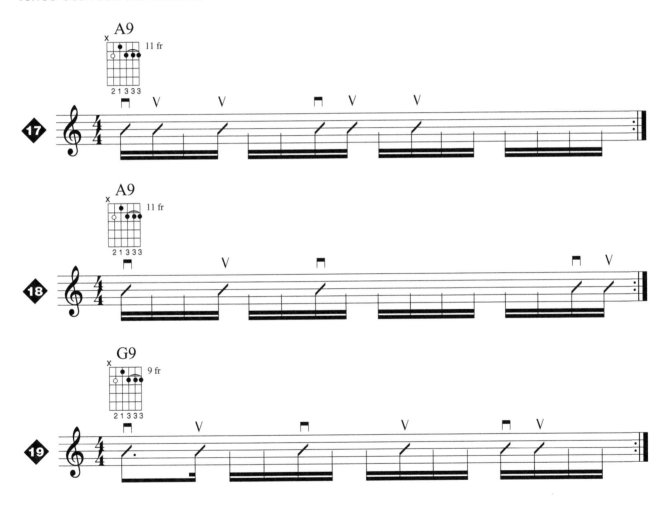

Now that you can play in time *without* the muted scratch, you should be aware that an occasional scratch sound between attacks can add a cool percussive effect to your funk playing. You may want to go back and play the examples on this page again. From this point onward, experiment and let your ears tell you how much of the scratch sound is appropriate.

5 The Swing Thing

Until now, all of our examples have had a "straight" feel. Let's begin playing some of the rhythms with a swing feel.

The swing groove happens by slightly delaying the second and fourth sixteenth of each beat. The best way to understand this is to hear it first. Listen to the audio, and then try it yourself: Simply scratch muted sixteenths with a straight feel, then stop and try the swing groove.

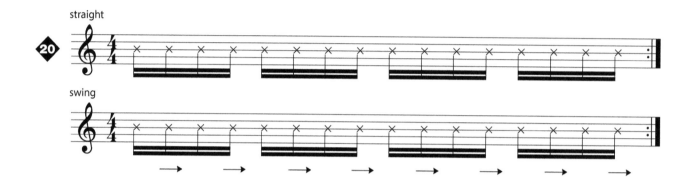

Play these familiar rhythm patterns with a swing feel. (Use our old reliable E9 chord.)

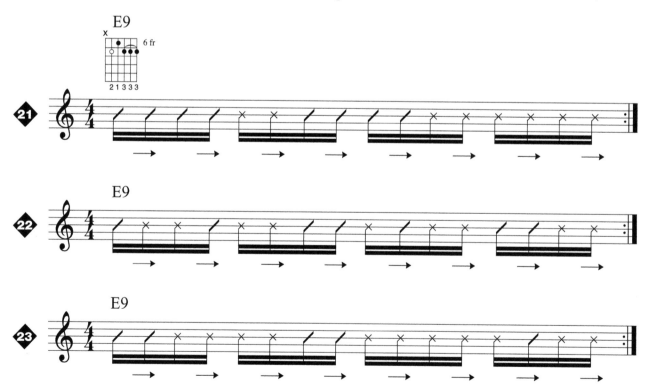

In funk, the swing feel can be used to varying degrees. You'll often see it notated like this: (♫ = ♩♪). Check out the following three swing jams. Each is a two-bar rhythm pattern.

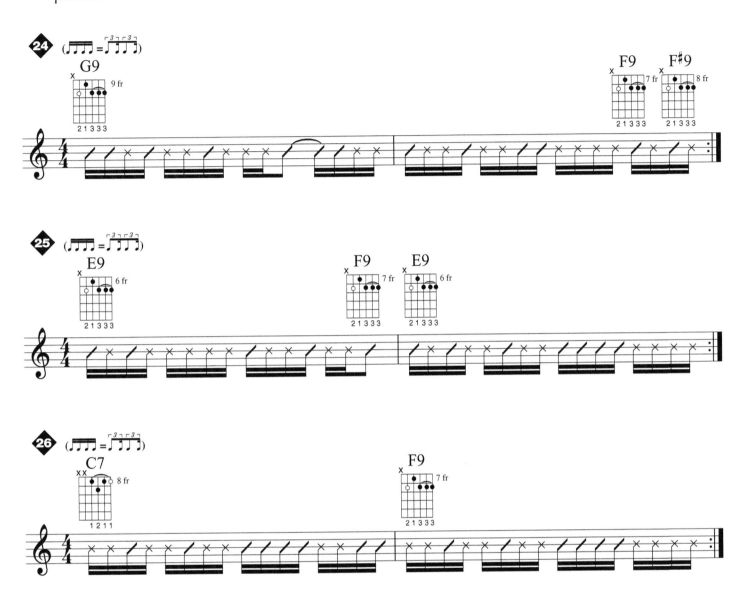

From this point on, some of the examples will have a swing feel and some will be straight.

6 Chords 'R' Us

Before moving into other funk techniques, let's take a moment to embellish the chords we've already played. By moving one note of a chord shape, we can enhance our rhythm parts, making them more melodic. (Remember that any of these shapes can be moved around the neck into different keys.)

The basic E9 shape is easily changed into an E13 chord. Use the following rhythm to practice alternating between these two shapes.

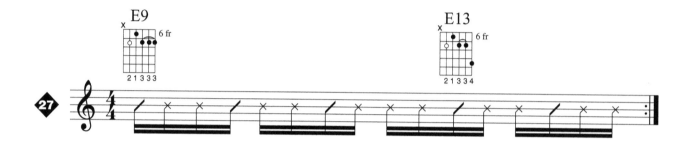

The other seventh chords we've used can also be modified by changing one note. These next embellishments are known as "sus4" (suspended fourth) or just "sus" chords. Play the following rhythms, alternating between these chord shapes.

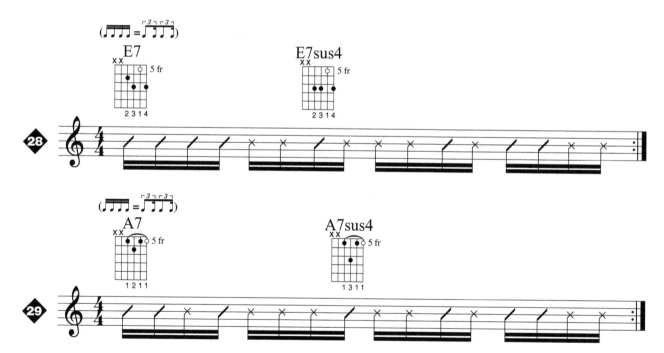

All the chords we've learned so far belong to a family known as "dominant" chords (more about that later). Here are some more chord shapes from that family, with embellishments. These two-bar patterns all feature a dominant chord (seventh or ninth) in the first measure and a "sus4" embellishment in the second measure.

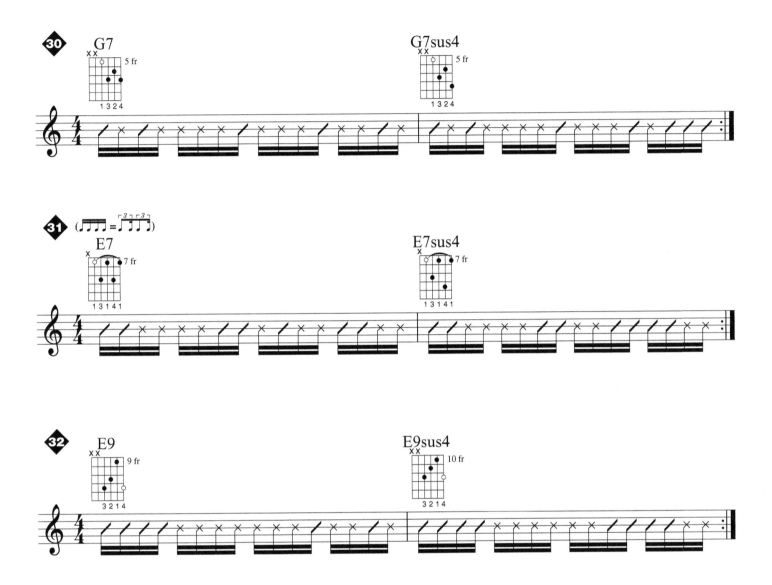

7 Slippery Slides

The half-step (one-fret) slide is a common trick that will add a little spice to your rhythm parts. Be aware of the following:

1. As you slide a chord, make sure the strings continue to ring. You don't want the notes of the chord to "die" as you slide.
2. The slide should be in time—just as if you were strumming the chord.
3. You may be tempted to stop your strumming hand as you slide, but keep "floating" those sixteenth notes.

Begin by just sliding the basic E9 shape from one fret below—strum an E♭9 chord, and slide your left hand up one fret, sounding the E9 without actually striking the strings. Are all the strings ringing?

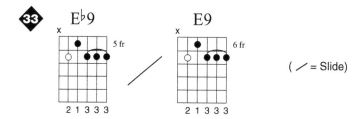

Now add the sixteenth scratch ("float" over the strings with your right hand during the slide).

Add two more attacks...

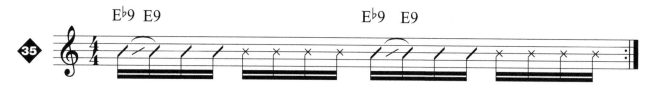

...and now, take one away.

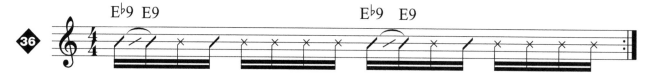

Here's a part with a slide and the thirteenth added.
(Remember the thirteenth chord shape?)

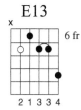

Now try sliding around with these two chord shapes.

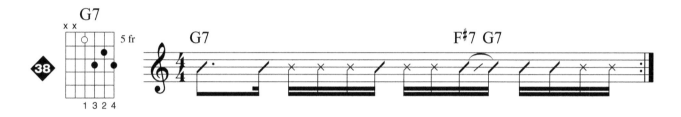

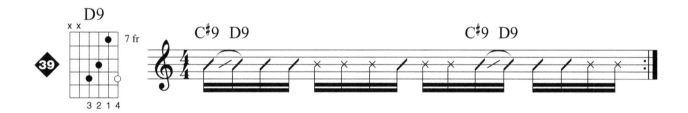

Of course, this slide technique can be used with any of the chords in the book.

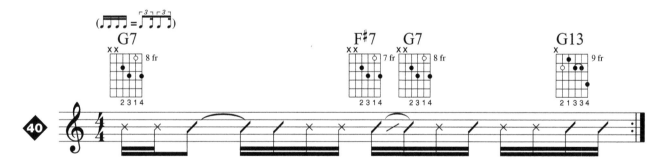

8 The Harmonic Rest Stop

As we build our funk technique, it seems like a good idea to pause and look at why we've been choosing these particular chords shapes and how they relate to each other on the fingerboard.

In the land of funk, most songs come from one of two harmonic families: dominant and minor. So far, we've been using dominant chords. Let's begin there.

Dominant Chords

Dominant chords are built from a major triad (1, 3, 5) with a lowered 7th (♭7). Extending the chord will give you more possibilities (9, 11, 13). You can also "alter" the extensions by raising or lowering them where appropriate (♭9, #9, #11, ♭13).

All of the chords we've played are common funk shapes. They fit into a logical order when viewed next to the guitar's fingerboard. These are known as chord "inversions."

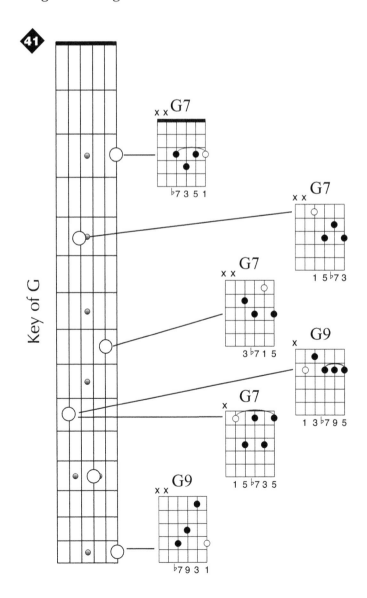

Minor Chords

Minor seventh chords are built from a minor triad (1, ♭3, and 5) with a lowered 7th (♭7). Like the dominant family, you can also "extend" the minor chords (9, 11, 13); however, unlike dominant, it's not appropriate to alter these extensions.

Compare the following diagram to the previous one, and you'll notice the similarities of the minor chords to the dominant shapes. (In most cases, the only difference is the third of the chord.) Feel free to go back and practice any of the previous examples in this book with their "parallel" minor chord shapes.

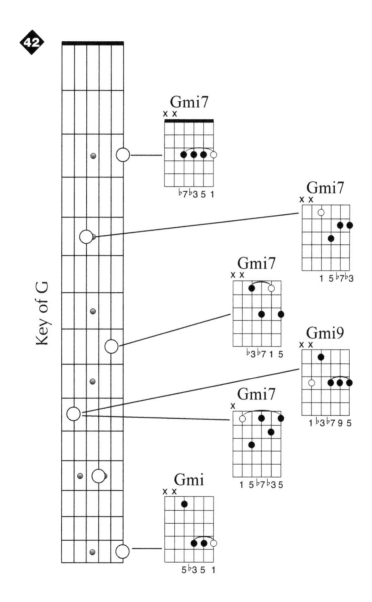

9 Scales

Later in the book we'll be playing some single-note funk parts, the notes of which are taken from scales relating to common funk harmony. The three scales most common to funk are *minor pentatonic, blues,* and *Mixolydian.* Although there are many ways to play each of these scales, for demonstration purposes, we'll limit our focus to two patterns each.

If these scales are new to you, try experimenting with them over the progressions shown. Notice that, like the chord diagrams, the roots of the scale have been highlighted. Any of these scale patterns can be moved around the neck to different keys.

Minor Pentatonic

We start with this scale because it's the most common. It has five notes rather than seven (typical of most scales) and is regularly used with dominant as well as minor chords.

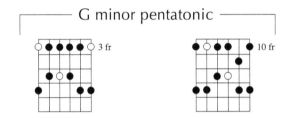

Try running up and down either of the above patterns (in the positions shown) over this progression in G minor. Jam, experiment, and have fun!

Blues

Like the minor pentatonic, the blues scale is also commonly used over dominant as well as minor chords. It is basically a minor pentatonic scale with one note added ($\flat$5).

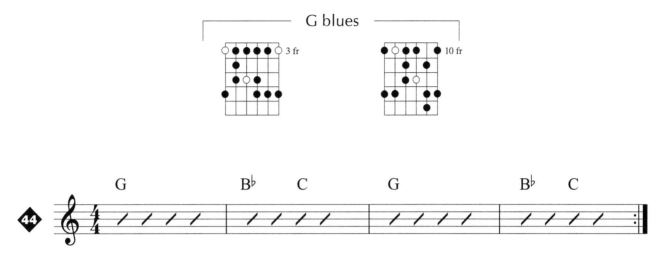

Mixolydian

This seven-note scale is directly related to dominant harmony. Unlike the other scales, its use is generally limited to dominant chords.

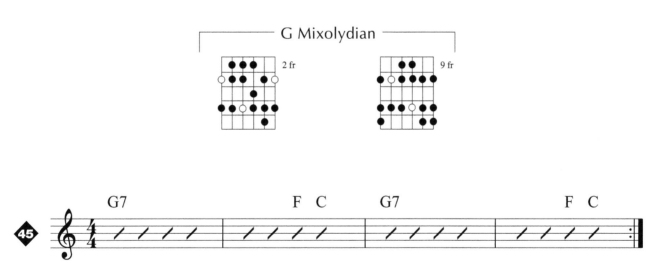

Please keep in mind that there are many other chord/scale options available to you! This is meant only as a general reference. Use this information as a place to start, and let your desire lead you deeper into the world of melody and harmony.

10 Minor Madness

Here are a few examples of how to apply minor chord shapes to funk rhythm patterns. Notice that in each of the following examples, a mini-melody is created by adding a note or two to the basic chord shape.

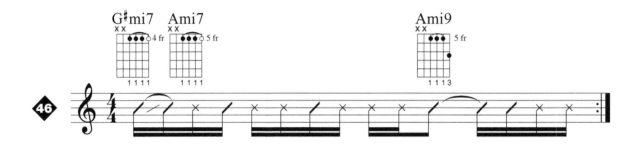

Don't let all the chord diagrams intimidate you; for the next two examples, you only need to move one finger for each new chord.

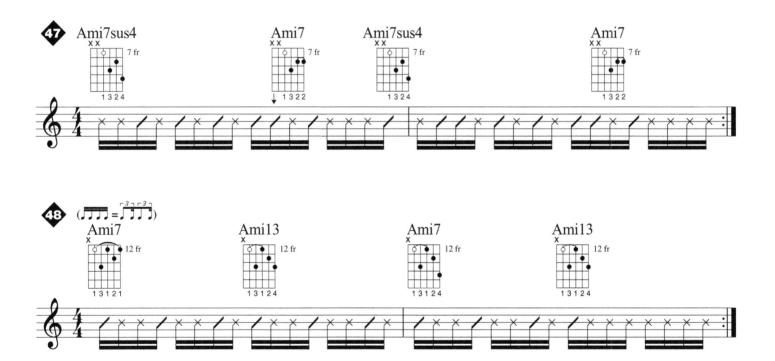

Here's a common minor chord progression, moving from the Imi chord (Ami) to the IVmi chord (Dmi).

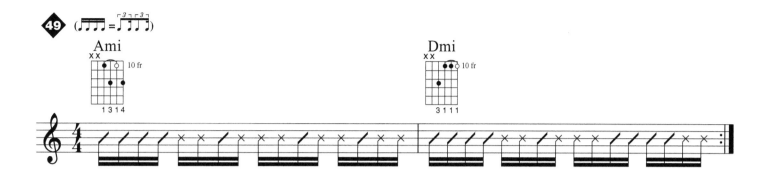

This one's way up high on the fretboard. Notice how much space is left at the end of the second measure. (Keep pumping that right hand!)

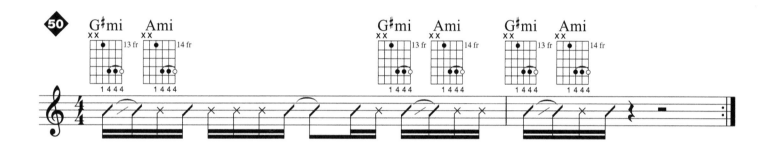

11 Get Picky With It

Many times, the best part for a groove is a simple single-note line. These parts are generally short, repeating ideas that use very few notes.

The first two examples below are *muted* parts. To get this sound, lightly rest the palm of your picking hand on the strings near the bridge. The pressure should be just enough to stop the sustain of the notes. To help you stay "in the pocket," keep your pick moving in sixteenths with the music.

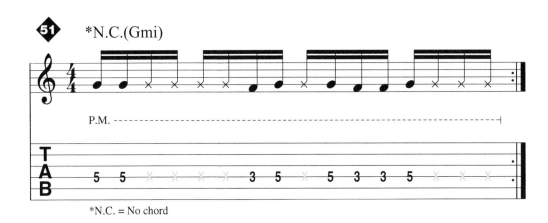

*N.C. = No chord

The next three grooves use a *skank* sound. This is the ultra-cool technique of isolating a single note while striking more than one string. This creates a big, percussive sound that really cuts through when the band is jamming. It can be difficult to execute (especially the upstrokes), so be patient.

Left hand: The trick is to mute the adjacent strings while fretting the note you want to hear.

Right hand: In general, scratch the note you want to hear along with one or two of the adjacent muted strings.

It's the muted strings in tandem with the single note that give you the chunky, "skank" tone. This first exercise should get you moving in the right direction.

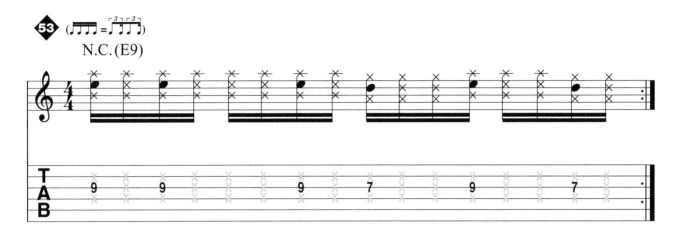

This part will definitely get you spankin' the skank.

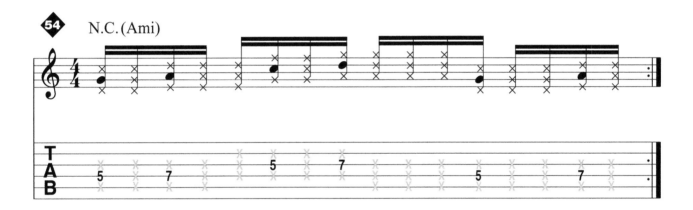

Here's a challenging part with more than enough upstrokes to confuse the groove. Try to "push" the B♭ up just a little to give this jam a bluesy sound.

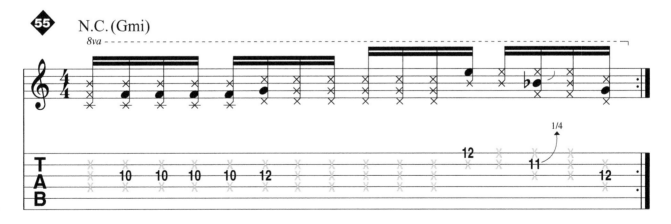

12 Throwin' Down

Now let's take what we've learned and create some real-life rhythm grooves. This first jam has two guitar parts (Guitar 1 is in the right channel, and Guitar 2 is in the left). The total length of the progression is eight bars: four on the E minor chords and four on the A dominant chords. Notice that the picking part (Gtr. 2) changes only one note as the chords change.

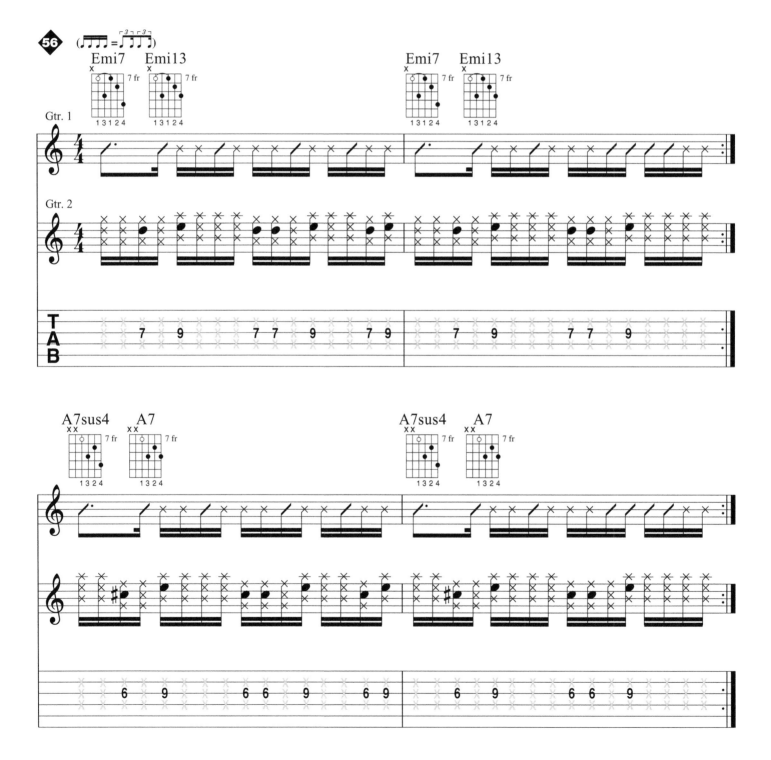

This two-bar groove also has two guitar parts. Guitar 1 basically stays on one chord, while Guitar 2 doubles the bass line.

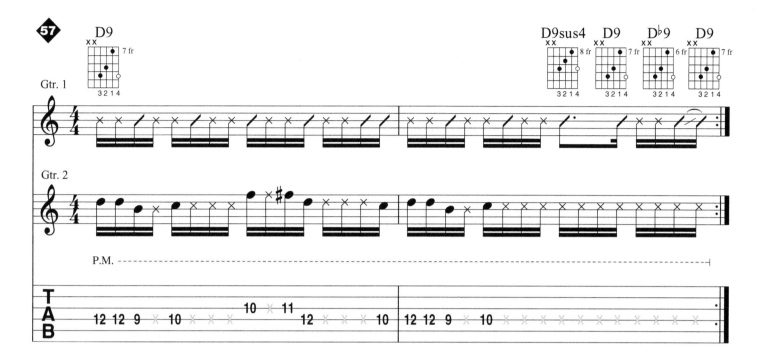

This single-guitar part moves up the neck quickly using chord inversions. Check out the half-step movement (B7–C7) in the second measure—this is *not* a slide.

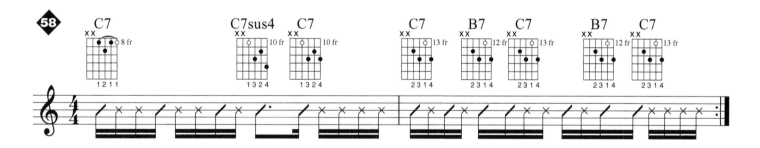

Here you're alternating between a skank part in the first measure and chords in the second measure.

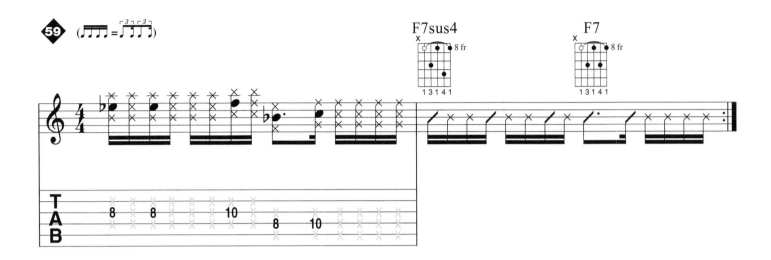

Now you're doing the job of two guitarists! You're slidin', you're skankin', you're playin' chord extensions—you're a freakin' funk machine!

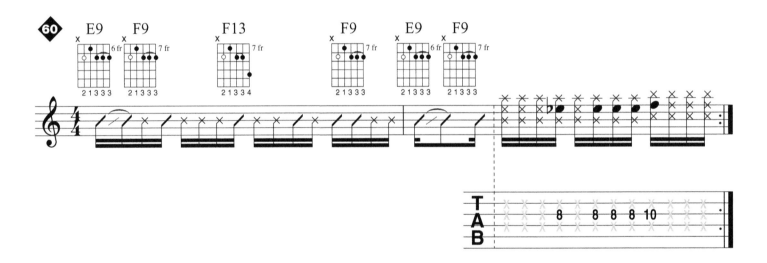

13 The Funky Shuffle

The *shuffle* is a common groove in many styles of music, and it can be found in funk as well. Up to this point, all of our grooves have had four sixteenth notes per beat. The shuffle we'll be playing here, however, has three eighth notes per beat. In musical terms, this is often referred to as a "12/8 groove" (4 beats x 3 eighth notes per beat).

This feel can be played many ways. Here's one approach. Notice that the strumming pattern begins with an upstroke. Although this can feel strange at first, it works because the backbeats (beats 2 and 4) are downstrokes and will eventually give you a stronger sense of time.

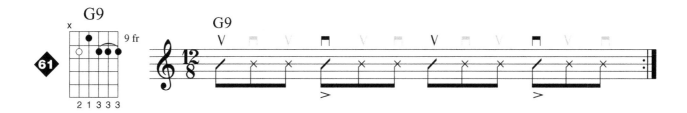

For this example, continue the same strumming pattern, but sustain the first note and "float" your hand over the second eighth note.

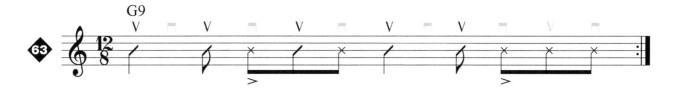

Let's expand the previous pattern by adding one attack on beat 2.

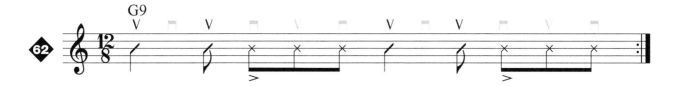

Finally, this two-bar pattern is based on a classic '70s funk shuffle. (Don't stop strumming over the A♭9 chord.)

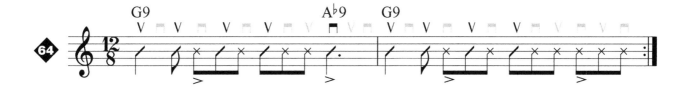

14 The End-of-the-Book, Just-for-Fun, Puttin'-It-All-Together, Party Jam!

This final jam includes many of the techniques discussed in the book. There are five sections; each one is eight bars long. We'll take at look at each section separately and then put them all together at a little faster tempo.

SECTION A: This first section is centered around the familiar E9 shape. The last chord jumps up the fretboard and may require some practice.

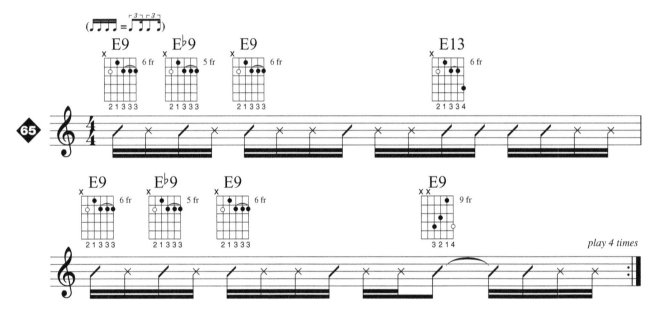

SECTION B: Now we move to the IV chord (A7). To create a melody on the top string, we base this section on three different inversions of the same chord.

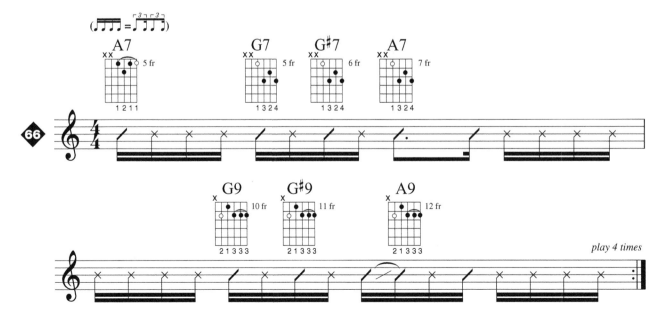

SECTION C: This is known as "the breakdown." The band hits on the first beat, and the guitar plays a single-note part with only the drums behind it. This repeats three times and then once again with the chords "walking up" to the next section.

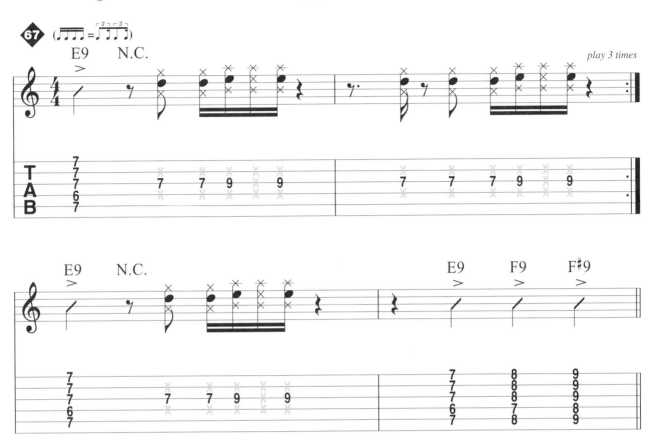

SECTION D: At this point, we've modulated into the key of G minor. This section might be called "the bridge." These chord shapes move around the neck, so take some time to get them under your fingers before playing with the track. This is a four-bar pattern that repeats once. The last chord leads you back into the next section.

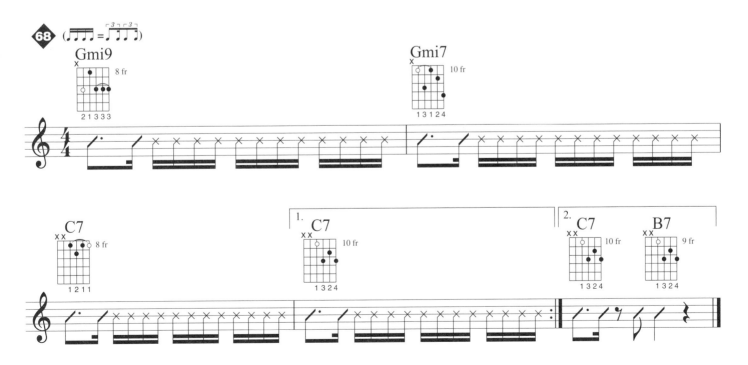

SECTION E: The last section brings us back to the key of E. The high voicing and six-teenth-note triplet give this part more intensity. Play this two-bar phrase four times with one final hit at the end.

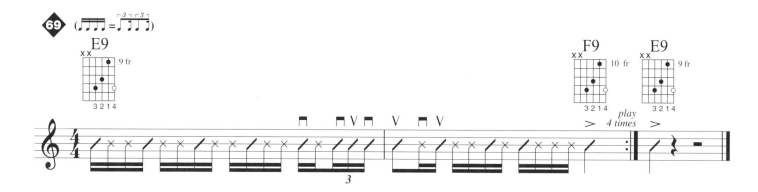

FYI: The sixteenth-note triplet can be an effective device for adding some flash to your playing. However, if overplayed, this little rhythmic trick can be annoying to your fellow bandmates, so use it sparingly!

PARTY JAM!—SECTIONS A, B, C, D, & E

Now it's time to put all the pieces together. This is meant to be challenging—so, if at first you don't succeed… have fun!